MEET THE GREATS

Anne FRANK

TIM COOKE

Gareth Stevens PUBLISHING

Please visit our website, www.garethstevens.com. For a free color catalog of all our high-quality books, call toll free 1-800-542-2595 or fax 1-877-542-2596.

Cataloging-in-Publication Data

Names: Cooke, Tim.
Title: Anne Frank / Tim Cooke.
Description: New York : Gareth Stevens Publishing, 2019. | Series: Meet the greats | Includes glossary and index.
Identifiers: LCCN ISBN 9781538225707 (pbk.) | ISBN 9781538225691 (library bound)
Subjects: LCSH: Frank, Anne, 1929-1945–Juvenile literature. | Jews–Netherlands–Amsterdam–Biography–Juvenile literature. | Jewish children in the Holocaust–Netherlands–Amsterdam–Biography–Juvenile literature.
Classification: LCC DS135.N6 C66 2019 | DDC 940.5318092 B–dc23

Published in 2019 by
Gareth Stevens Publishing
111 East 14th Street, Suite 349
New York, NY 10003

For Brown Bear Books Ltd:
Editorial Director: Lindsey Lowe
Managing Editor: Tim Cooke
Children's Publisher: Anne O'Daly
Design Manager: Keith Davis
Designer and illustrator: Supriya Sahai
Picture Manager: Sophie Mortimer

Concept development: Square and Circus / Brown Bear Books Ltd

Picture Credits: Front Cover: Character artwork, Supriya Sahai. Interior: 20th Century Fox: 42; Dreamstime: Ronald Jansen, 8; General Dutch Photographers Agency: Ben van Meerendonk, 20; Getty Images: Ann Frank Fonds Basel/Frans Dupot, 31; istockphoto: adisa, 10; Knopf Doubleday: 41; Public Domain: 32, 33, Blacknight, 38, Collecite Anne Frank Stichting Amsterdam, 12, Google Sites/Jewish Virtual Library, 29, IOC Olympic Museum Switzerland, 18, MGM, 25b, Karya Sendiri, 24b, Smithsonan.com/ Smithsonian mag, 30; Robert Hunt Library: 9, 13, 14, 15, 21, 28 34; Shutterstock: BESTWEB, 43, Adam Boor, 35, Glyn, 39, Ronald Wilfred Jansen, 40, Igor Stramyk, 11b, Naci Yavuz, 22; Topfoto: Fine Art Images/Heritage Images 23b, The Granger Collection 11t, 25t.

CPSIA compliance information: Batch #CS18GS. For further information contact Gareth Stevens, New York, New York at 1-800-542-2595.

Contents

Introduction

Anne Frank died during World War II (1939–1945), before she was 15. Yet today her name is known around the world.

Anne was one of the six million Jews and millions of others killed by the **Nazis** in the **Holocaust**. Anne is one of the best known of the victims because she kept a diary as a teenager. Anne wrote down her thoughts while she was in hiding with her family in a secret apartment behind her father's office in Amsterdam. The family was trying to avoid being arrested by the Nazis. Shortly before the war ended, they were discovered and sent to **concentration camps**. Anne, her older sister, Margot, and their mother all died.

Anne's father, Otto, survived and returned to Amsterdam. Anne's diary had been saved, and Otto believed it should be published so that everyone would understand what had happened to ordinary people during the war. Today, the book has sold more than 30 million copies.

Clouds GATHER

Anne's early life was happy. No one knew her life would end so tragically. However, political change was starting to sweep through Germany.

Annelies Marie Frank was born in Frankfurt, Germany, on June 12, 1929. She was never known as Annelies—her family always called her Anne. Anne's sister, Margot, was three years older. The family was Jewish and lived very comfortably in Frankfurt. Otto Frank was a businessman and Anne's mother, Edith, stayed home to look after her daughters with the help of a nanny. Otto had served in the German army in World War I (1914–1918). Germany had been defeated, and many Germans felt the country had been punished too harshly by the victors. This feeling would have terrible consequences.

QUICK FACTS

- Anne Frank was born to a Jewish family in Germany.
- The family fled Germany because the Nazi government was **persecuting** Jews.

The Franks were forced to leave their apartment in Frankfurt in 1931.

AN INNOCENT CHILDHOOD

In 1931, when Anne was almost two years old, the family's landlord asked them to leave their apartment in Frankfurt. He supported the Nazi Party, which was growing politically powerful in Germany. The party's leader, Adolf Hitler, promised to restore Germany. More than 500,000 Jews lived in Germany, and Hitler blamed them for the defeat in World War I and for Germany's economic problems. He encouraged **prejudice** and **discrimination** against Jews.

MOVING HOME

Otto Frank moved his family to another part of Frankfurt. The new neighborhood was full of children, and Anne and Margot spent hours playing outdoors with their friends. Anne was much naughtier than Margot, who was quiet and enjoyed studying.

As Hitler's power increased in Germany, Otto decided to leave. In 1933, the family moved to Switzerland, then later that year, Otto moved to Amsterdam, capital of the Netherlands. The rest of the family joined him in January 1934.

The Nazis staged **militaristic** parades to show off their power.

LIFE IN AMSTERDAM

The Franks joined many other German Jews who had moved to the Netherlands. The Dutch had a reputation for being welcoming to foreigners. Otto also chose Amsterdam because he already spoke Dutch. The family moved into a new apartment and Otto started a new business.

Anne and Margot went to the local school, where they were taught in Dutch. Soon, they could speak the language fluently. They made lots of friends. There were many other children at school whose families had escaped from Germany. Only Edith Frank found their new life difficult.

Downtown Amsterdam had many canals lined with old homes.

Otto and Anne Frank on a family day out.

FAMILY FUN

Anne loved Amsterdam. It was a fun place to grow up. She enjoyed riding her bike along the city canals with her friend Hannah. When the canals froze in winter, the girls went ice-skating on them. The beach was not far away, and one summer, the Frank family vacationed at the seaside in neighboring Belgium. Anne was a good swimmer. Otto took many photographs of his two daughters on their vacations. Some of these photographs still survive.

Anne loved to cycle along the canals of Amsterdam.

Anne enjoyed school, but her teachers said she talked too much.

A LIVELY GIRL

At school, Anne loved writing and learning about history and the myths of ancient Greece. Her least favorite subject was math. She was very popular with her classmates and her teachers, although some of the teachers complained that she talked too much in class! Anne was also mischevious. She liked to play pranks, such as pouring water on visitors' heads from the balcony of the Frank family's apartment. She loved seeing the suprised looks on their faces.

GERMAN INVASION

In September 1939, Germany invaded Poland, beginning World War II. The following spring, Germany began to attack its western neighbors. On May 10, 1940, German airplanes bombed Amsterdam as German troops invaded the Netherlands. Thousands of Dutch people were killed. The Dutch surrendered on May 15. The Netherlands was now an **occupied** country. Speaking to her people by radio from London, the Dutch queen told them not to panic. For the Franks and many other people, that was difficult.

German troops arrive in Amsterdam during the occupation of the Netherlands in May 1940.

The Rise of THE NAZIS

When World War I ended in 1918, Germany was blamed for starting the conflict. The victors forced Germany to pay huge fines, called reparations.

The reparations almost bankrupted Germany. In the 1920s, unemployment rose and high inflation wiped out the value of people's savings. Germans resented the terms of the peace treaties that had ended the war. An ambitious politician named Adolf Hitler appealed to the people's resentment. He promised to make the nation powerful again.

Hitler's Nazi Party gained support in the 1920s. It was based on military-style discipline and loyalty to Hitler. In 1933, the Nazis won elections and Hitler maneuvered his way to become the leader of Germany. He ruled as a **dictator**.

Hitler had been a soldier in World War I. He ran Germany in a militaristic style.

The Nazis rose to power by persuading millions of Germans to vote for them.

Hitler blamed German Jews for Germany's defeat in World War I. He also persuaded many Germans that Jewish businessmen had undermined the economy. The Nazis began to persecute the Jews in 1933. Soon they began to imprison Jews in concentration camps. Later, Nazi leaders came up with the "Final Solution." This was a plan to murder all of the Jews in German-occupied Europe.

Jewish prisoners at Dachau, the first concentration camp, which opened in 1933.

Under OCCUPATION

Following the Nazi invasion of the Netherlands, the Frank family found their lives in Amsterdam changing rapidly.

The Nazi invasion meant that it was too late for Anne and her family to escape from the Netherlands. A few Jewish people did manage to flee, but the Frank family had no car, and Anne's grandmother, who lived with them, was too old and sick to travel anywhere. The Franks had come to Amsterdam to escape from the Nazis—but now the Nazis had arrived and the Franks were stuck in their adopted home. The Nazis began imposing their authority on the Netherlands. The distinctive Nazi **swastika** flag soon flew from public buildings across Amsterdam.

QUICK FACTS

- After the German occupation, life became dangerous for Jews living in the Netherlands.
- To save his family, Otto Frank decided to go into hiding.

LIFE CHANGES

Life changed for everyone in the Netherlands, but mainly for Jewish people. Every Jewish person, including children like Anne and Margot, had to register their names and addresses with the Germans. The Jews were the only group of people who had to do this.

The Nazis then seized all businesses owned by Jews. Otto had protected his business by legally giving it to two non-Jewish colleagues to look after. The Nazis banned people from reading books written by Jewish authors, and Jews could no longer go to the movies. Anne loved the movies and had pictures of movie stars on her bedroom walls. To get around the ban, Otto and Edith rented movies to show at home. Anne even made tickets to give out to the friends they invited to watch the movies with them.

Anne had a poster in her bedroom of Sonja Henie, a Norwegian ice-skater who became a movie star.

A GENERAL STRIKE

The position of Jews in the Netherlands worsened dramatically on February 22, 1941. The Nazis arrested several hundred Jews living in Amsterdam. The Jews were forced onto trains and taken away to concentration camps, where they were murdered. Many people had heard rumors about camps where people were killed or forced into slave labor. The removal of the Jews from Amsterdam seemed to confirm these terrible stories.

A poster seeking Dutch recruits for the German armed forces.

Outraged at what had happed, the Dutch staged a **general strike** on February 25. The Netherlands came to a standstill. It was the first time that an occupied people had resisted their Nazi occupiers in such a way. The Dutch sent a clear signal that they did not agree with their Nazi governors.

THINGS WORSEN

The strike made no impression on the Nazis. If anything, life became tougher for Jews. Signs were put up in the city's museums, restaurants, libraries, and zoo, and even on park benches, forbidding Jews to use them. Jews could no longer use public beaches and pools.

The general strike only made things worse for Dutch Jews.

Although things were getting more difficult for Amsterdam's Jewish population, the Franks tried to carry on life as normal. In summer 1941, Anne could not go to the beach for her summer vacation, so she went to the countryside with the family of her friend, Sanne. Another normal event that summer was the wedding of Otto's assistant at work, Miep. Miep was not Jewish—and she would play a very important part in the life of the Frank family.

Nazi supporters closed down Jewish stores and other businesses.

SEGREGATION

The end of the summer brought more changes. Anne was told that she could no longer attend school with non-Jews, only with Jewish children. At least she and her friend Hannah were in the same class. Then, in April 1942, the Nazis announced that all Jews over the age of six must wear a yellow star on their clothes to show that they were Jewish. The star had to be worn so it could be clearly seen. This made it easier for the Nazis to enforce more new rules forbidding Jews to ride bikes—they were already banned from driving—or leave their homes in the evening.

Jews had to wear a yellow star based on the Star of David, a Jewish symbol.

FAMILY CRISIS

On June 12, 1942, Anne celebrated her 13th birthday with her friends. It was the last party she would have. Her favorite gift was a small notebook from her father. It was a diary with a green-and-red checked cover and a clasp. Anne named the diary "Kitty," for a friend. She wrote her first entry two days after her birthday, on June 14.

Less than a month later, Margot received a letter ordering her to a labor camp in Germany. Instead, Otto told the girls to pack a few possessions. The girls had no idea where they were going. They put on several layers of clothes under their raincoats and set off walking in the pouring rain. Anne took her precious diary with her.

A SECRET HOME

The family walked 3 miles (5 km) to Otto's office in Amsterdam. Unknown to Anne and Margot, Otto and Edith had secretly been planning this move since Otto's application to move the family to the United States had been turned down in 1941.

For months, Otto and Edith had gradually been moving possessions into a secret **annex** hidden above Otto's office. They had moved in furniture, including a stove, as well as supplies of food. The Franks had tried to be careful so they didn't arouse the suspicion of the Nazis. The family moved into their secret home in the annex on July 6, 1942.

Anne's diary became her most treasured possession.

The Hidden ANNEX

The Frank family's new home was hidden behind a bookcase in Otto's office. No one could see the apartment from the outside.

The annex was several small rooms hidden behind a secret door. The bookcase swung open to reveal a steep staircase that led up to two rooms and a bathroom. One of the rooms had a sink and a stove for cooking. On the floor above were two tiny bedrooms, one for Otto and Edith and one for the girls. Anne's parents had decorated the girls' room with Anne's pictures of movie stars. The living space was just 450 square feet (41.8 sq m). It became even more cramped when another Jewish family, the van Pels, also moved in with the Franks.

The annex was at the top of one of the two houses that made up Otto's offices.

The kitchen in the annex was also used as a bedroom.

The annex had curtains over the windows so that nobody could see in from outside. During the day, the family could not make any sound at all. They could not even flush the toilet or turn on the faucet. They even had to argue without shouting—and there were lots of arguments in such a confined space. Anne was shocked that the adults argued so much. Some of the arguments were about Anne herself. The van Pels thought that she was very spoiled.

Anne's posters included the film star Greta Garbo.

Family in HIDING

The Franks hid in the annex for more than two years. Anne recorded her most private thoughts in her beloved diary, "Kitty."

When the Frank family went into hiding in July 1942, they had no idea how long they would have to stay in their new home. The United States had entered the war in December 1941, and the Franks hoped that meant Hitler would soon be defeated. Life would not be easy until then. A week after the Franks arrived in the annex, they were joined by another Jewish family they knew: the van Pels, and their 15-year-old son, Peter. Five months later, a Jewish dentist named Fritz Pfeffer also moved in. Space was so limited that Anne and Fritz had to share a room.

QUICK FACTS

- Anne, her family, and four other people lived in the secret annex for 25 months.
- No one knows if someone betrayed them to the Germans or if they were found by accident.

DAY AFTER DAY

Everyone found life in the annex boring. During the day, Anne, Margot, and Peter spent a lot of time studying with Otto. Anne still did not like math! They also studied history, geography, foreign languages, and literature. The children hoped to go back to school when the war was over, and none of them wanted to be behind. The families followed the progress of the war by listening to radio broadcasts from London. At night, they could hear **Allied** bombers overhead flying to bomb Germany.

Anne was frightened by the noise of bombers, but Otto told her that bombing Germany would shorten the war.

Anne shared her bedroom with Fritz Pfeffer.

A WELCOME VISITOR

Otto and Edith had stored as much tinned food as they could in the annex before they moved in. The food soon ran out, and the families needed some fresh food too. Miep Gies, Otto's assistant, was one of the only people who knew about the annex, and she wanted to help her friends. Each day, Edith wrote a grocery list and Miep brought food. Miep had to be careful. If she bought too much food, it might raise suspicions, so she only bought a little extra for the people in the annex. She also bought newspapers and books so Anne and the others could follow the progress of the war. Anne especially loved hearing news about her friends.

DOOMED ROMANCE

Anne was lonely in the annex. She poured all her feelings into her diary. She and Margot were not close, and Anne did not get along well with their mother. Otto was her favorite family member. Anne and Peter van Pels grew close. They were similar in age, and Anne liked spending time with him. On April 1, 1944, she wrote in her diary, “I’d love to lay my head on his shoulder and just sit there quietly.” Peter kissed her two weeks later. Anne was so happy!

Anne stuck photos of herself into her diary.

Margot (left) and Anne did not share their feelings very much.

A CLOSE CALL

Everyone in the annex lived in fear of discovery. Anne wrote that they were "as quiet as baby mice." In April 1944, burglars broke into the business downstairs. Workers who did not know about the annex called the police. The police searched the building and found the bookcase. Someone had left a light on in the annex behind it—but the police did not notice. The close escape shook everyone up. The families drew up new rules to make sure that they were not careless again.

DISCOVERED

On the morning of August 4, 1944, Peter heard men's voices downstairs in the office. The men demanded to know where the Jews were hiding. The next thing, German secret police called **Gestapo** climbed up the narrow staircase into the annex. Even today, no one knows how the Nazis had found out about the hidden families. Some people believe that someone must have reported hearing sounds or seeing lights from the annex. Other people think that the families were betrayed by one of the few trusted people who knew they were in hiding.

The Gestapo told Anne and the other occupants of the annex to pack their valuables. One of the police picked up a briefcase in which Anne's diary, notebooks, and other writings were stored. The contents fell out onto the floor. As the families were marched away, nobody picked the papers up.

Peter van Pels died in a concentration camp a year after being taken from the annex.

Did someone betray the location of the annex behind the bookcase to the Germans?

A FAMILY DESTROYED

As the families left the annex, a Gestapo officer asked Otto how long they had been in hiding. He did not believe Otto's reply that they had been there for two years. To prove that he was not lying, Otto pointed to the wall where he had recorded Anne's height over the previous two years.

As Anne walked out of the office downstairs, it was the first time she and the others had been outside for over two years. It was also one of the last times the Frank family would ever be together.

Concentration CAMPS

By the time the occupants of the annex were arrested, the Nazis had built an extensive network of prison camps throughout Europe.

The camps were called concentration camps because the Nazis could "concentrate" very large numbers of prisoners into a small area. The majority of prisoners were Jews. The prisoners also included political opponents, homosexual people, disabled people, Roma people, and others.

The first camps were like prisons. Inmates were fed poorly and forced to carry out slave labor. People died from exhaustion and sickness. From 1941, the Nazis began building new death camps.

Prisoners were kept in dirty, overcrowded camps.

Gas chambers at Auschwitz were disguised as shower blocks.

The death camps were part of the "Final Solution," the Nazi plan to **exterminate** the Jews. Hundreds of thousands of Jews from occupied Europe were packed into cattle trucks and taken by train to camps, such as Auschwitz in Poland. People who were unable to work were killed with gas. The others were used for slave labor. If they became too weak to work, they were killed. Up to 6,000 people a day were murdered at camps such as Auschwitz and Bergen–Belsen, in northern Germany.

Rumors about the purpose of the concentration camps spread through Europe during the war. When they were discovered, Anne and her family knew the fate that awaited them. Historians think that more than three million people were murdered in the death camps.

A Famous DIARY

Otto was the only member of the family to survive the war. When he discovered Anne's diary, he decided the world needed to read it.

Once the occupants of the annex had been discovered, there was little doubt about what would happen to them. The Germans sent all Dutch Jews they captured to concentration camps. About 106,000 Dutch Jews died in the camps. Overall, about 75 percent of all the Jews living in the Netherlands at the start of the war were killed by the Nazis—the highest proportion of Jewish deaths in any country in Western Europe. The Franks, the van Pels, and Fritz Pfeffer were held in Amsterdam for four days before they were loaded into cargo trucks and moved out of the city by train.

QUICK FACTS

- Anne Frank died in Bergen-Belsen in March 1945.
- After the war, Otto Frank read her secret diary and decided it should be published.

A TERRIBLE JOURNEY

The train first took Anne and the others to Westerbork, a camp northeast of Amsterdam. They were held there for a month before being taken to the concentration camp at Auschwitz in Poland. The family reached Auschwitz in early October 1944. When they arrived, the prisoners were separated into two groups. One group, including Mr. van Pels, was sent straight to the gas chambers and killed. The people who were fit to work, which included Anne, went into the camp.

The remains of Westerbork camp in the Netherlands.

Rail lines terminate at the station at Auschwitz.

AT AUSCHWITZ

Otto Frank and the other men were split up from their families. Anne, Margot, and their mother were marched into the women's section of the camp. Their heads were shaved, they were given a sacklike dress to wear, and a number was tattooed on their arms. They were given almost nothing to eat but had to work in the fields all day. Soon, Anne and Margot got sick with **scabies**.

A marker in remembrance of Anne and Margot on the site of the Bergen–Belsen camp.

REACHING THE END

Anne and Margot were soon sent to another camp at Bergen–Belsen. Edith and Otto Frank remained in Auschwitz. Edith became ill with a high fever and died on January 6, 1945, from starvation.

Conditions for Anne and Margot in Bergen–Belsen were appalling. There was little food or **sanitation** and many prisoners had **typhus**, a disease that causes diarrhea and fever. Anne and Margot had to work as they grew weaker from typhus. Margot died early in March 1945. Anne died a few days later. On April 15, British troops **liberated** the camp.

RETURN TO AMSTERDAM

Auschwitz had been liberated by Soviet troops on January 27, 1945. Otto Frank was in the hospital, but was still alive. Early in May, Hitler killed himself, and Germany surrendered, ending World War II. Otto returned to Amsterdam in June 1945. He was met by Miep Gies and her husband. Otto already knew Edith had died in Auschwitz, but he hoped Anne and Margot might have survived. He found out in October that they had both died.

Miep had a surprise for Otto. She had saved the papers and notebooks from the floor of the annex—including Anne's diary. She told Otto they were Anne's gift to him. Reading the diary was heartbreaking for Otto. The entries brought Anne's sparkling personality back to life. Otto decided to type up the diaries for his mother and other friends to read. They were so moved that they urged him to publish the diary so that others could read the remarkable account.

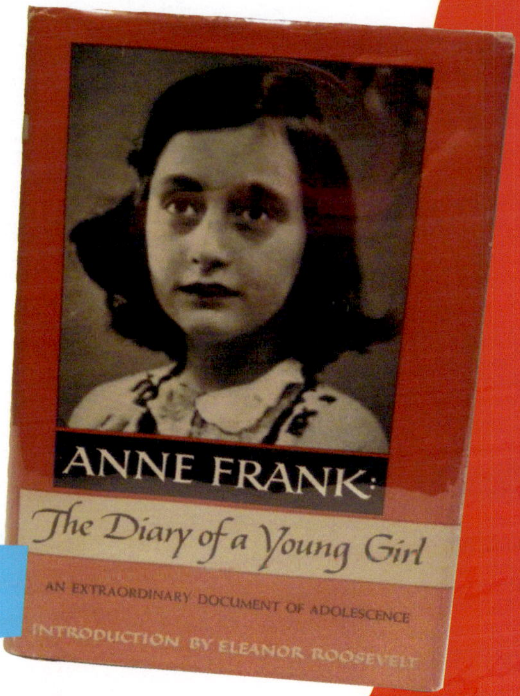

Eventually, Otto decided to have Anne's diary published.

GLOBAL BEST SELLER

Otto decided that Anne's story should be told so that people could understand what had happened to the Jews and the impact of the Holocaust. At first, he took out some personal details from the diary, but he decided that they were important and put them back. The book was published in Dutch in the summer of 1947 as *The Secret Annex*. It sold out almost at once. Later, the title was changed to *Anne Frank: The Diary of a Young Girl*.

Millie Perkins and Joseph Schildkraut as Anne and Otto Frank in the movie *The Diary of Anne Frank* (1959).

A LASTING SYMBOL

The Nazis had killed more than six million Jews and millions of other people. Around 1.5 million Jewish children had died. Such a crime was difficult to fully understand, but Anne's story helped to reveal its personal side. It helped people to understand the real and lasting effects of the **genocide**.

Otto Frank lived until 1980. He dedicated the rest of his life to making sure that Anne became a powerful symbol of the tragic cost of life in war. Today, Anne Frank is one of the most famous teenagers to have ever lived. The secret annex where the families hid is one of the most visited tourist sites in Amsterdam.

A statue of Anne Frank was put up near the secret annex in 1977.

Timeline

1929

- Born in Frankfurt, Germany, on June 12.

1933

- Adolf Hitler becomes chancellor of Germany, where his Nazi Party begins to persecute Jewish citizens.
- Otto Frank moves his family to Switzerland, and then to Amsterdam.

1934

- Anne, her sister, and their mother join Otto in Amsterdam in January.

1940

- German forces occupy the Netherlands on May 10.

1941

- German **authorities** in Amsterdam transport the first Dutch Jews to concentration camps.
- The Dutch hold a general strike to show their disapproval of the Germans' action.
- In the summer, Anne and her family attend the wedding of Otto's assistant, Miep Gies.

1942

- Anne celebrates her 13th birthday with a party on June 12. Her father gives her a diary, which Anne names "Kitty."
- After Margot receives a letter ordering her to go to a labor camp, the family goes into hiding on July 6.
- The van Pels family moves into the annex on July 13.
- A dentist named Fritz Pfeffer also moves into the annex.

1944

- A burglary in the office next door almost leads to the discovery of the annex.
- On August 4, the Gestapo finds the annex and arrests all of the occupants.
- Anne and the others are transported to Auschwitz in Poland. Anne and Margot are moved on to a camp at Bergen–Belsen.

1945

- Otto Frank is freed from Auschwitz in January by Soviet troops.
- Anne Frank dies from typhus early in March, a few days after her sister Margot.
- On June 3, Otto Frank returns to Amsterdam. He knows his wife has died but is hopeful that his daughters might have survived.
- Otto receives news in October that Anne and Margot have died. Miep Gies gives him the diary she had been saving to return to Anne.

1947

- The diary is published under the title *The Secret Annex*.

KEY PUBLICATIONS AND MOVIES

- *Diary of a Young Girl (book, 1947)*
- *Tales from the Secret Annex (book, 1949)*
- *The Diary of Anne Frank (movie, 1959)*
- *The Attic: The Hiding of Anne Frank (TV movie, 1988)*
- *Anne Frank Remembered (TV movie, 1995)*
- *The Diary of Anne Frank (TV movie, 2009)*

Glossary

Allied In World War II, relating to the side led by the United States, Great Britain, and the Soviet Union.

annex A building joined on to a main building to provide additional space.

authorities Representatives of the government.

concentration camps Prison camps in which large numbers of people are held in a relatively small area.

dictator A ruler with complete control over a country.

discrimination The unfair treatment of a group of people based on their race, religion, or other factors.

exterminate To destroy a population completely.

general strike A strike carried out simultaneously by workers in all or nearly all industries.

genocide The killing of a large number of people because of their nationality or ethnicity.

Gestapo The state secret police of Nazi Germany.

Holocaust The campaign of mass murder carried out by the Nazis in Europe.

liberated Set someone free from imprisonment or slavery.

militaristic Organized on military lines, and promoting an aggressive military policy.

Nazis The National Socialist Party that governed Germany from 1933 to 1945.

occupied Controlled by an invading army or other organization.

persecute To treat people harshly, often because of their race or religious beliefs.

prejudice A negative feeling toward something or someone that is not based on reason or experience.

sanitation The process of keeping places clean.

scabies A contagious skin disease that causes red spots and severe itching.

swastika A symbol of a cross with its four arms broken at right angles.

typhus An infectious fever spread by lice, insects, and fleas.

Further Resources

Books

Abramson, Ann. *Who Was Anne Frank?* New York: Grosset & Dunlap, 2007.

Agrimbau, Diego. *Anne Frank.* Mankato, MN: Capstone Press, 2017.

Burling, Alexis. *Anne Frank: Holocaust Diarist.* Minneapolis, MN: Essential Library, 2016.

Editors of LIFE. *Anne Frank: The Diary at 70: Her Life and Her Legacy.* New York: LIFE, 2017.

Throp, Claire. *The Horrors of the Holocaust.* Chicago: Heinemann Raintree, 2017.

Websites

Anne Frank House
www.annefrank.org/
The website of the Anne Frank House in Amsterdam, with many details about Anne's life.

Anne Frank Center for Mutual Respect
http://annefrank.com/about-anne-frank/diary-excerpts/
A selection of extracts from Anne's famous diary.

BBC History
www.bbc.co.uk/annefrank/timeline.shtml
A timeline of Anne's life.

Spartacus Educational
spartacus-educational.com/GERfrankA.htm
A detailed biography of Anne, with many quotations from the diary.

Publisher's note to educators and parents: Our editors have carefully reviewed these websites to ensure that they are suitable for students. Many websites change frequently, however, and we cannot guarantee that a site's future contents will continue to meet our high standards of quality and educational value. Be advised that students should be closely supervised whenever they access the Internet.

Index